No Quick Fix

Examining Human Body Systems

Student Activities

Second Edition

A Problem–Based Learning Unit Designed
for 6th–8th Grade Learners

CENTER FOR GIFTED EDUCATION
THE COLLEGE OF WILLIAM & MARY

KENDALL/HUNT PUBLISHING COMPANY
4050 Westmark Drive   Dubuque, Iowa 52002

Book Team
Chairman and Chief Executive Officer: *Mark C. Falb*
President and Chief Operating Officer: *Chad M. Chandlee*
Director of National Book Program: *Paul B. Carty*
Editorial Development Manager: *Georgia Botsford*
Developmental Editor: *Lynnette M. Rogers*
Vice President, Operations: *Timothy J. Beitzel*
Assistant Vice President, Production Services: *Christine E. O'Brien*
Senior Production Editor: *Charmayne McMurray*
Permissions Editor: *Renae Horstman*
Cover Designer: *Jenifer Chapman*

Author Information for Correspondence and Workshops:
Center for Gifted Education
The College of William and Mary
P.O. Box 8795
Williamsburg, VA 23187-8795
Phone: 757-221-2362
Email address: *cfge@wm.edu*
Web address: *www.cfge.wm.edu*

Center for Gifted Education Staff, First Edition
Project Director: Dr. Joyce VanTassel-Baska
Project Managers: Dr. Shelagh A. Gallagher
Dr. Victoria B. Damiani
Project Consultants: Dr. Beverly T. Sher
Linda Neal Boyce
Dana T. Johnson
Dr. Donna L. Poland
Dr. Jill D. Burruss

Center for Gifted Education Staff, Second Edition
Executive Director: Dr. Joyce VanTassel-Baska
Director: Dr. Elissa F. Brown
Curriculum Director and Unit Editor: Dr. Kimberley L. Chandler
Curriculum Writers: Dr. Janice I. Robbins
Dr. Kimberly Tyler
Dr. Kimberley L. Chandler
Curriculum Reviewer: Dr. Beverly T. Sher

The William and Mary Center for Gifted Education logo is a depiction of the Crim Dell Bridge, a popular site on the William and Mary campus. Since 1964, this Asian-inspired structure has been a place for quiet reflection as well as social connections. The bridge represents the goals of the Center for Gifted Education: to link theory and practice, to connect gifted students to effective learning experiences, to offer career pathways for graduate students, and to bridge the span between general education and the education of gifted learners.

Contents

Glossary

Agar A semisolid gel containing nutrients; used in Petri dishes as a food source and support for colonies of microorganisms

Antibody Antibodies are immune system molecules produced by B lymphocytes. These molecules bind to foreign antigens, allowing other components of the immune system, such as macrophages, to recognize the antibody-coated foreign particles as threats to the body and remove them. The body makes billions of different kinds of antibody molecules, each of which is capable of recognizing only a small number of foreign antigens. This diversity allows the body the flexibility necessary to respond to essentially any foreign antigen it may encounter.

Antigen A substance that can cause immune system cells to react and produce a specific immune response aimed at removing it from the body. Antigens can be fragments of bacteria, viruses, cancer cells, or (unfortunately) normal body cells.

Assumption A conclusion based on one's own beliefs and presuppositions

Autoclave A device that uses heat and pressure to kill microorganisms and sterilize materials and equipment

B Lymphocyte (B Cell) The immune system cell type responsible for producing antibodies

Bacilli Rod-shaped bacteria

Biotic A living component of the environment, includes animals and plants

Biotic and Abiotic Input Both living and nonliving components that are considered "inputs" from areas outside the boundaries of the system (such as animals that immigrate, sunlight, rain, pollutants)

Bone Marrow The tissue of the human immune system in which B cells develop; also contains cells known as stem cells, which are the precursors for all cell types found in the blood. Bone marrow is found in cavities in the centers of bones, such as the long bones of the legs.

Boundary Something that indicates or fixes a limit on the extent of the system

Constant The factor or factors in an experiment that are kept the same and not allowed to vary

Control The part of an experiment that serves as a standard of comparison. A control is used to detect the effects of factors that should be kept constant, but that vary.

Dependent Variable The factor or variable that may change as a result of changes purposely made in the independent variable

Dysfunctional Describing something that is not working properly

Element (of a System) A distinct part of the system; a component of a complex system (a subsystem)

Epidemiology A science that deals with the incidence, distribution, and control of a disease in a population

Functional Describing something that is working properly

Generalization A general statement about all members of a class or group

Granulocyte A white blood cell that contains granules that stain with various dyes; involved in defenses against bacteria

Hilar Lymphadenopathy Swelling of the lymph nodes located in the hilum (the area between the lungs that contain the blood vessels that carry blood between the lungs and the heart); according to the Merck manual, this is the most common finding in children with TB.

Histology The study of the microscopic structure of the body's tissues and organs; concerned with relating structure and function

Hypothesis A tentative explanation for an observation, phenomenon, or scientific problem that can be tested by further investigation

Immunodeficient Deficient in immune function. An immunodeficient person will be unable to produce a normal immune response when challenged by a foreign antigen and will therefore be more susceptible to infectious disease. Immunodeficiency can be caused by many different things, including poor nutrition, stress, genetic defects, infection with certain viruses (including HIV, the virus that causes AIDS), and cancer chemotherapy.

Implication A suggestion of likely or logical consequence; a logical relationship between two linked propositions or statements

Independent Variable The variable that is changed on purpose by the experimenter

Inference Act of reasoning from factual knowledge or evidence; interpretation based on observation

Input (to a System) Something that is put in the system; an addition to the components of the system

Interaction Connection made between/among elements and inputs of a system

Interdependent Mutually relying on or requiring the aid of one another

Isoniazid A drug used in the treatment of tuberculosis

Lymph Tissue fluid containing lymphocytes and other white blood cells that circulates between the tissues and the blood through the lymphatic system

Lymph Node Located in many parts of the body, lymph nodes are organs of the immune system that filter the lymph. Macrophages within the nodes trap foreign antigens (such as bacteria and viruses) and allow the other cells of the immune system to mount an effective immune response against them. These organs are also known (somewhat inaccurately) as lymph "glands".

Lymphocyte The white blood cell type responsible for carrying out specific immune responses. B cells and T cells are lymphocytes.

Macrophage A large phagocytic cell (one that takes up particles by surrounding them with its membrane, much as an amoeba does); macrophages in the immune system trap foreign antigens and then display them on their cell surfaces in a form that can be recognized by lymphocytes. Macrophages are also responsible for removing foreign particles once they have been coated by antibodies, as well as for killing bacteria.

Monocyte Immune system macrophage found in the blood

Mycobacterium tuberculosis (M. tuberculosis) A rod-shaped bacterium (bacillus) that causes tuberculosis (Tuberculosis can also be caused by two other related species of bacteria, *M. bovis* and *M. africanum.*)

Output (from a System) Something that is produced by the system; a product of the system interactions

Pathogen A specific causative agent of a disease (such as a bacterium or virus)

Perspective An attitude, opinion, or position from which a person understands a situation or issue

Productive Effective in achieving specified results

Reasoning The process of forming conclusions, judgments, or inferences from facts or premises

Rifampin A drug used in the treatment of tuberculosis

Spleen A long, slender organ of the immune system that lies in the center of the body near the liver; filters the blood, and traps foreign particles in order to allow the immune system to mount effective immune responses against viruses and bacteria traveling in the blood; also recycles aging red blood cells and recovers the iron in them

Stakeholder A person who has an interest in or involvement with an enterprise or issue and its potential outcomes

Strain of Bacteria A subgroup within a bacterial species caused by genetic variation. For example, *M. tuberculosis* bacteria that are genetically resistant to the effects of isoniazid are members of a resistant strain of *M. tuberculosis.*

System A group of interacting, interrelated, or interdependent elements forming a complex whole

T Lymphocyte (T Cell) T cells are lymphocytes that develop in the thymus. They are responsible for killing virally infected cells (a process managed by the killer T cells, which are usually CD8+ T cells) and for regulating the development of immune responses (a process carried out by helper T cells, which are CD4+ T cells). CD4+ T cells are also responsible for an immune process called *delayed-type hypersensitivity.* This process is the basis of the tuberculin test: CD4+ T cells in people who have previously been infected with TB will react to the tuberculosis antigens injected into their skin and cause a red, swollen lump to develop at the site of the injection.

Thymus The immune system organ in which T cells develop; located in the upper part of the chest near the heart

Tuberculosis A chronic, recurrent infection, often of the lungs, but any organ may be infected; one of the major causes of human suffering and death throughout history

For other terminology relating specifically to tuberculosis, visit the Centers for Disease Control website at http://www.cdc.gov/tb/faqs/qa_glossary.htm.

Laboratory Safety Precautions

As this unit involves laboratory work, some general safety procedures must be observed at all times. Most school districts have prescribed laboratory safety rules; for those that do not, some basic rules to follow for scientific experimentation are:

1. Students must behave appropriately in the lab. No running or horseplay should be allowed; materials should be used for only the intended purposes.

2. No eating, drinking, or smoking in lab; no tasting of laboratory materials.

3. If students are using heat sources, such as alcohol burners, long hair must be tied back and loose clothing should be covered by a lab coat.

4. Fire extinguishers should be available; students should know where they are and how to use them.

5. A specific safety rule relevant to implementing this unit is that when culturing bacteria, students should not open Petri plates that have grown bacteria or fungal colonies: infection or allergic reactions may result. Seal Petri plates with masking tape or Parafilm before allowing students to analyze them.

_____   _____
Student Signature   Date

_____   _____
Teacher Signature   Date

Name _____ Date _____

Content Pre-Assessment

1. a. Why is tuberculosis especially dangerous to people who are immunodeficient?

   b. List two groups of people who are especially at risk if they become infected with tuberculosis.

2. a. How does the tuberculin test work?

   b. Is the tuberculin skin test a good way to find out if someone has active tuberculosis? Why or why not?

continued

3. Describe the functions of each of the following immune system cells:

a. B cells

b. T cells

c. Macrophages

Name _____   Date _____

Experimental Design Pre-Assessment A

Construct a fair test of the following question: Is a certain strain of bacteria resistant to ampicillin, a common antibiotic?

Describe in detail how you would test this question. Be as scientific as you can as you write about your test. Write the steps you would take to find out if a certain strain of bacteria is resistant to ampicillin.

Adapted from Fowler, M. (1990). The diet cola test. *Science Scope, 13(4),* 32–34.

Name   Date

Experimental Design Pre-Assessment B

You have asthma, a chronic disease that makes you cough (which is annoying but not necessarily serious) and makes it hard to breathe (which is serious); severe asthma attacks can be life threatening. Most of the time, you have no problems and manage to get by without using bronchodilators (drugs that expand the size of your breathing passages and relieve your asthma symptoms). You are very allergic to ragweed: ragweed pollen makes your asthma much worse. During ragweed season, which typically lasts about 6 weeks where you live, you find that you need to use bronchodilators much more frequently. Your biggest problems are at night: the inhaled bronchodilator that you use at bedtime wears off by about 2:00 A.M., and so you wake up coughing, have to take another dose from your inhaler, and then have trouble getting back to sleep. Your allergist suggests that you try an oral form of the medication that may take longer to wear off. She cautions you not to use the oral form during an acute asthma attack, though, because it takes 20 minutes to start working, whereas your inhaled bronchodilator only takes a few seconds. How can you decide which form of the medication works best for you at night during ragweed season?

1. Describe an experiment that would allow you to choose between the two. In your answer, include the following:

   a. Your hypothesis

   b. The materials you would need (including any necessary safety equipment)

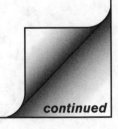

continued

c. The protocol you would use

d. A data table showing what data you would collect

e. A description of how you would use your data to decide whether the oral form of your bronchodilator works better than the inhaled form

Name _____   Date _____

Systems Pre-Assessment

A classroom can be thought of as a system.

1. List the parts of the system in the spaces provided. Include boundaries, elements, inputs, and outputs.

   Boundaries:

   Elements:

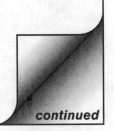

continued

Inputs:

Outputs:

2. Draw a diagram of the system that shows where each of the parts can be found.

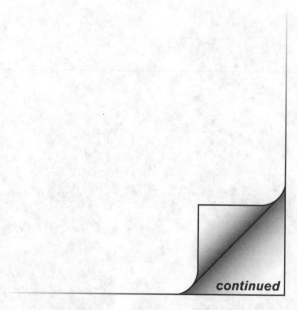

continued

3. On your diagram, draw lines (in a different color) showing three important interactions between different parts of the classroom system. Why is each of these interactions important to the system? Explain your answer.

   a. Interaction 1

   b. Interaction 2

   c. Interaction 3

Name _____   Date _____

Initial Problem Statement

You are Dr. Susan Ostrovsky. You have been trained as a physician, and also have a master's degree in public health. You did your residency in infectious diseases and are now on staff at the Eastbridge Public Health Department. This morning, you received the following e-mail message from your boss, who is away at an important training program in Washington, D.C.

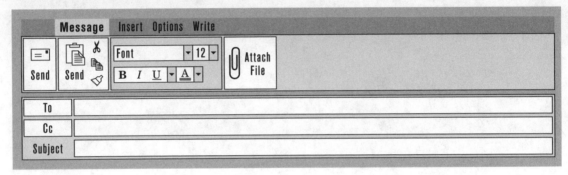

Susan:

Dr. Johnston (from Eastbridge Pediatrics) called yesterday afternoon to inform us that one of his patients, a 15-year-old boy, has been confirmed as having active tuberculosis. The boy had a positive tuberculin test 2 weeks ago. A sputum smear was positive for acid-fast bacilli.

Dr. Johnston has referred the patient to Dr. Goldstein at University Hospital for treatment.

Please follow up on this as soon as possible. The patient is a student at Eastbridge High School. As you know, the school is terribly overcrowded and the potential for a serious outcome is great.

I need an action plan from you by tomorrow morning. Please fax it to me at my hotel in Washington, D.C. The training lasts another three weeks, so I'll need daily updates from you until I get back.

Marvin Jones, M.D., Director
Eastbridge Public Health Department

Name _____ Date _____

Need to Know Board

What we know . . .	What we need to know . . .	How we can find out . . .

Name   Date

Additional Problem Statement Information

Memo

From Dr. Johnston:

The patient is 15-year-old Todd Miller. He had a negative tuberculin test a year ago and a positive tuberculin test 2 weeks ago. Sputum tests revealed the presence of acid-fast bacteria. He has been referred to Dr. Goldstein, an infectious disease specialist at University Hospital, for treatment.

The tuberculin test was given as a part of a physical exam required for participation in the high school swim team.

His parents and two younger brothers were given tuberculin tests 2 days ago; we will pass along the results when they become available.

Name   Date
_____

Additional Problem Statement Information

MEMO

From Dr. Goldstein:

Todd Miller has a positive tuberculin skin test and positive sputum tests. Thus, he has active tuberculosis and should be considered potentially infectious. Culture results are not yet available. Lateral chest X-rays have revealed the presence of hilar lymphadenopathy. Two days ago, I started him on isoniazid and rifampin; barring any complications, this treatment should continue for 9 months.

Name _____   Date _____

Problem Log Questions

1. What do you think the problem is now?

2. Why do you think this is the main problem?

3. What are the issues you are most interested in finding out about, and why?

Name _____ Date _____

Additional Problem Statement Information

 Telephone message from Earl Smith, principal of Eastbridge High School:

Mr. Smith is very concerned about the situation and eager to help. Needs the text of a letter to parents explaining the situation and recommending appropriate action. Would be willing to open the school to any necessary health department response.

Name   Date

Information from Todd Miller's Parents

Todd has two younger brothers, Jason (age 11) and Michael (age 4).

      Jason attends Eastbridge Middle School.

      Michael attends the Eastbridge Community Preschool.

Todd recently spent 2 months in New York City living with his uncle Jim who is a policeman. Jim Miller's wife Sarah is a nurse at one of the large teaching hospitals in New York City. They have no children. Todd and his uncle spent the summer exploring the city; he was not involved in group programs with other children.

Todd is active in swimming and diving. He is also involved in the Boy Scouts and his church youth group.

Our primary care physician is Dr. Carlson, with Eastbridge Clinical Partners.

Name _____   Date _____

Information from Dr. Johnson

Todd's two younger brothers have both had positive tuberculin skin tests. I have referred them to Dr. Goldstein for follow-up.

Name _____ Date _____

Information from Dr. Carlson

Both Mr. and Mrs. Miller's tuberculin tests were negative. We will continue to monitor this situation.

Name _____ Date _____

Health Department Action Plan

1. Briefly describe the situation that requires action.

2. Why must the health department become involved in this situation?

3. What must be done? Give a good reason for each recommended action. Use another sheet if necessary.

Action	Reason
a.	
b.	
c.	

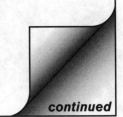

continued

4. Who outside the health department must be involved in the proposed activities? List people to contact and their roles in this plan. Use another sheet if necessary.

      <u>**Person**</u>   <u>**Role**</u>

a.

b.

c.

Name _____ Date _____

Systems Diagram

Name of System _____

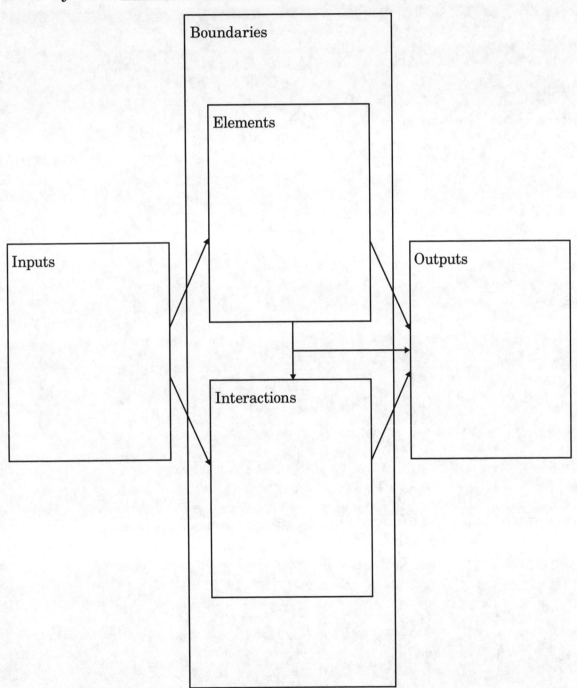

Boundaries

Elements

Inputs

Outputs

Interactions

Name _____   Date _____

Systems Model

Name of System _____

Give examples of how the system demonstrates each generalization.

The interactions and outputs of a system change when its inputs, elements, or boundaries change.
Systems can be productive or dysfunctional.
Many systems are made up of smaller systems.
Systems are interdependent.
All systems have patterns.

Name _____   Date _____

System Parts Chart

1. What are the boundaries of the system? Why did you choose them? Were there other possibilities?

2. List some important elements of the system.

3. Describe inputs into the system. From where do they come?

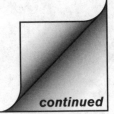

continued

4. Describe outputs from the system. What parts of the system produce them?

5. Describe some important interactions:

   a. among system elements

   b. between system elements and inputs into the system

6. What would happen to the system if the interactions in Question 5a could not take place? In Question 5b?

Name _____   Date _____

Article: "The Immune System"

The Body's First Line of Defense

The immune system is a complex of organs—highly specialized cells and even a circulatory system separate from blood vessels—all of which work together to clear infection from the body.

The organs of the immune system, positioned throughout the body, are called lymphoid organs. The word "lymph" in Greek means a pure, clear stream—an appropriate description considering its appearance and purpose.

Lymphatic vessels and lymph nodes are the parts of the special circulatory system that carries lymph, a transparent fluid containing white blood cells, chiefly lymphocytes.

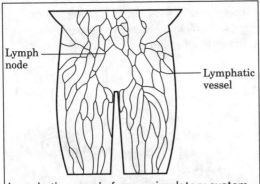

Lymph node

Lymphatic vessel

Lymphatic vessels form a circulatory system that operates in close partnership with blood circulation.

Lymph bathes the tissues of the body, and the lymphatic vessels collect and move it eventually back into the blood circulation. Lymph nodes dot the network of lymphatic vessels and provide meeting grounds for the immune system cells that defend against invaders. The spleen, at the upper left of the abdomen, is also a staging ground and a place where immune system cells confront foreign microbes.

Pockets of lymphoid tissue are in many other locations throughout the body, such as the bone marrow and thymus. Tonsils, adenoids, Peyer's patches, and the appendix are also lymphoid tissues.

Both immune cells and foreign molecules enter the lymph nodes via blood vessels or lymphatic vessels. All immune cells exit the lymphatic system and eventually return to the bloodstream. Once in the bloodstream, lymphocytes are transported to tissues throughout the body, where they act as sentries on the lookout for foreign antigens.

Source: http://www.niaid.nih.gov/final/immun/immun.htm.
National Institute of Allergy and Infectious Disease, a division of the National Institutes of Health: NIAID Office of Communications and Public Liaison, 6610 Rockledge Drive, MSC 6612, Bethesda, MD 20892-6612; http://www3.niaid.nih.gov/

continued

How the Immune System Works

Cells that will grow into the many types of more specialized cells that circulate throughout the immune system are produced in the bone marrow. This nutrient-rich, spongy tissue is found in the center shafts of certain long, flat bones of the body, such as the bones of the pelvis. The cells most relevant for understanding vaccines are the lymphocytes, numbering close to 1 trillion.

The two major classes of lymphocytes are B cells, which grow to maturity in the bone marrow, and T cells, which mature in the thymus, high in the chest behind the breastbone.

B cells produce antibodies that circulate in the blood and lymph streams and attach to foreign antigens to mark them for destruction by other immune cells.

B cells are part of what is known as antibody-mediated or humoral immunity, so called because the antibodies circulate in blood and lymph, which the ancient Greeks called, the body's "humors."

Certain T cells, which also patrol the blood and lymph for foreign invaders, can do more than mark the antigens; they attack and destroy diseased cells they recognize as foreign. T lymphocytes are responsible for cell-mediated immunity (or cellular immunity). T cells also orchestrate, regulate, and coordinate the overall immune response. T cells depend on unique cell surface molecules called the major histocompatibility complex (MHC) to help them recognize antigen fragments.

Organs and tissues of the immune system dot the body in a protective network of barriers to infection.

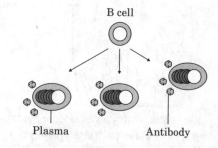

B cells become plasma cells, which produce antibodies when a foreign antigen triggers the immune response.

Antibodies

The antibodies that B cells produce are basic templates with a special region that is highly specific to target a given antigen. Much like a car coming off a production line, the antibody's frame remains constant, but through chemical and cellular messages, the immune system selects a green sedan, a red convertible, or a white truck to combat this particular invader.

continued

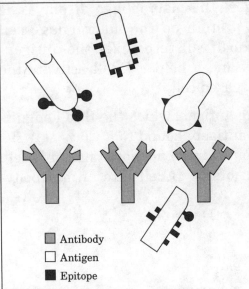

▨ Antibody
☐ Antigen
■ Epitope

Antibodies produced by cells of the immune system recognize foreign antigens and mark them for destruction.

Resting T cell

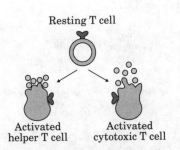

Activated helper T cell Activated cytotoxic T cell

T lymphocytes become CD4+ or helper T cells, or they can become CD8+ cells, which in turn can become killer T cells, also called cytotoxic T cells.

However, in contrast to cars, the variety of antibodies is very large. Different antibodies are destined for different purposes. Some coat the foreign invaders to make them attractive to the circulating scavenger cells, phagocytes, that will engulf an unwelcome microbe.

When some antibodies combine with antigens, they activate a cascade of nine proteins, known as complement, that have been circulating in inactive form in the blood. Complement forms a partnership with antibodies, once they have reacted with antigen, to help destroy foreign invaders and remove them from the body. Still other types of antibodies block viruses from entering cells.

T Cells

T cells have two major roles in immune defense. Regulatory T cells are essential for orchestrating the response of an elaborate system of different types of immune cells.

Helper T cells, for example, also known as CD4 positive T cells (CD4+ T cells), alert B cells to start making antibodies; they also can activate other T cells and immune system scavenger cells called macrophages and influence which type of antibody is produced.

Certain T cells, called CD8 positive T cells (CD8+ T cells), can become killer cells that attack and destroy infected cells. The killer T cells are also called cytotoxic T cells or CTLs (cytotoxic lymphocytes).

Immune System Process

After it engulfs and processes an antigen, the macrophage displays the antigen fragments combined with a Class II MHC protein on the macrophage cell surface. The antigen-protein combination attracts a helper T cell and promotes its activation.

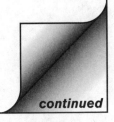

continued

After a macrophage engulfs and processes an antigen, the macrophage displays the antigen fragments combined with a Class I MHC protein on the macrophage cell surface. A receptor on a circulating, resting cytotoxic T cell recognizes the antigen-protein complex and binds to it. The binding process and a helper T cell activate the cytotoxic T cell so that it can attack and destroy the diseased cell.

A B cell uses one of its receptors to bind to its matching antigen, which the B cell engulfs and processes. The B cell then displays a piece of the antigen, bound to a Class II MHC protein, on the cell surface. This whole complex then binds to an activated helper T cell. This binding process stimulates the transformation of the B cell into an antibody-secreting plasma cell.

Activation of Helper T Cells

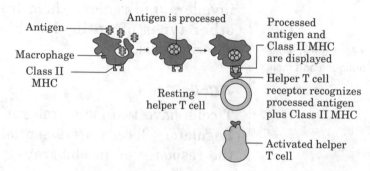

Activation of Cytotoxic T Cells

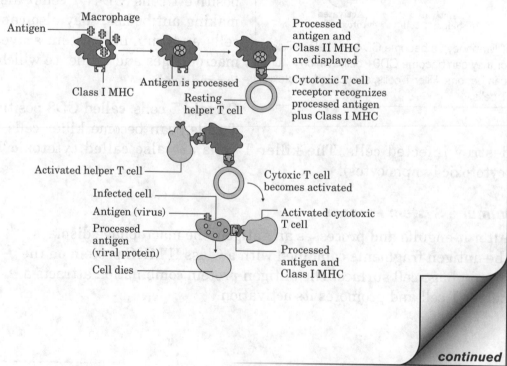

continued

Activation of B Cells to Make Antibody

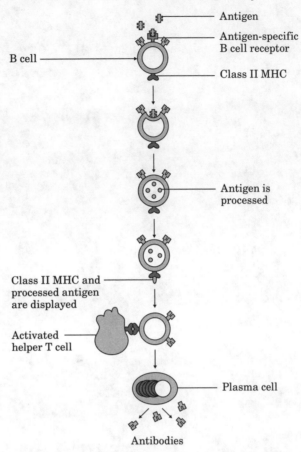

Antigen

Antigen-specific
B cell receptor

B cell

Class II MHC

Antigen is
processed

Class II MHC and
processed antigen
are displayed

Activated
helper T cell

Plasma cell

Antibodies

Name _____   Date _____

Histology Worksheet

1. Observe the prepared slide of blood cells. Draw each cell type that you see; using the histology atlas, identify as many of the cell types that you see as possible. Label your drawings. Can you find and draw red blood cells? Monocytes? Granulocytes? Lymphocytes? Which cell type seems to be most abundant in the blood? Which immune system cell type seems to be most abundant in the blood?

2. Observe the prepared slide of the thymus cells. Draw a picture of what you see. Use the histology atlas to help identify the different structures and cells that you see. Label your diagram appropriately. What appears to be the predominant cell type in this organ?

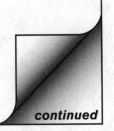

continued

3. Observe the prepared slide of the spleen cells. Draw a picture of what you see. Use the histology atlas to help identify the different structures and cells that you see. Label your diagram appropriately. What appears to be the predominant cell type in this organ?

4. Observe the prepared slide of the lymph node cells. Draw a picture of what you see. Use the histology atlas to help identify the different structures and cells that you see. Label your diagram appropriately. What appears to be the predominant cell type in this organ?

Name   Date

System Parts Chart

1. What are the boundaries of the system? Why did you choose them? Were there other possibilities?

2. List some important elements of the system.

3. Describe inputs into the system. From where do they come?

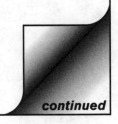

continued

4. Describe outputs from the system. What parts of the system produce them?

5. Describe some important interactions:

   a. among system elements

   b. between system elements and input into the system

6. What would happen to the system if the interactions in Question 5a could not take place? In Question 5b?

Name   Date

Systems Diagram

Draw a picture of the system. Show where its boundaries are. Label and describe all of its parts.

Problem Log Questions

Name _____ Date _____

1. For the system you considered, what was the main effect of *M. tuberculosis* infection? Is this a serious problem for the system? Why or why not?

2. Did considering the system you looked at as a system help you to understand tuberculosis better? Why or why not?

Name _____   Date _____

Reasoning Wheel

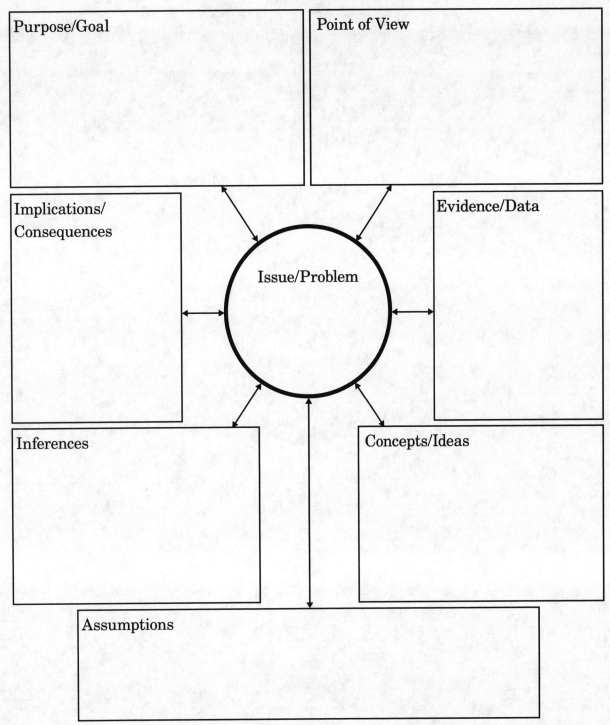

Purpose/Goal

Point of View

Implications/
Consequences

Evidence/Data

Issue/Problem

Inferences

Concepts/Ideas

Assumptions

Adapted from Paul, R. (1992). *Critical thinking: What every person needs to survive in a rapidly changing world.* Sonoma, CA: Foundation for Critical Thinking.

Name _____ Date _____

Article: "Tuberculosis Still a Threat"

By Christy Feig
CNN Medical Unit

NEWARK, New Jersey (CNN)—Tuberculosis rarely crosses the minds of most Americans. Maybe that's because cases of the disease have been declining for more than a century.

But experts from the Centers for Disease Control and Prevention (CDC) are gathering in Atlanta this week to discuss—among other things—the importance of keeping their guard up when it comes to infectious diseases like TB.

There were 16,000 cases of TB registered in the United States last year. That's still a decline but the numbers are leveling off. What concerns researchers is the fact that some newer strains of TB are resistant to standard treatments. And these strains are spreading.

"TB changed my life drastically, I haven't worked in four years," says one patient who wishes to remain anonymous. He has a resistant strain of TB and is left with one option—have part of his lung removed.

Smaller World, Likelier Spread

Rebecca Stevens keeps a close eye on such patients as part of an aggressive program in New Jersey.

She watches each patient swallow each dose of medicine—the only way to contain TB. "Most of my patients take medicine for at least 18 months," she says.

She also voices concern about the severity of the disease. "TB is a community disease, one person with TB can make a million people sick," she says.

And lots of time spent in tight spaces—like prisons, hospitals and poverty-stricken neighborhoods—can aid in the spread of TB.

Although resistant strains of TB are more common in countries outside the United States, experts say increased travel is making our world smaller—and making the international spread of resistant tuberculosis more likely.

From CNN.com, March 16, 2002 by Christy Feig. Copyright © 2002 by Cable News Network, LP. Reprinted by permission.

Name _____   Date _____

Reasoning About a Situation or Event

What Is the Situation?

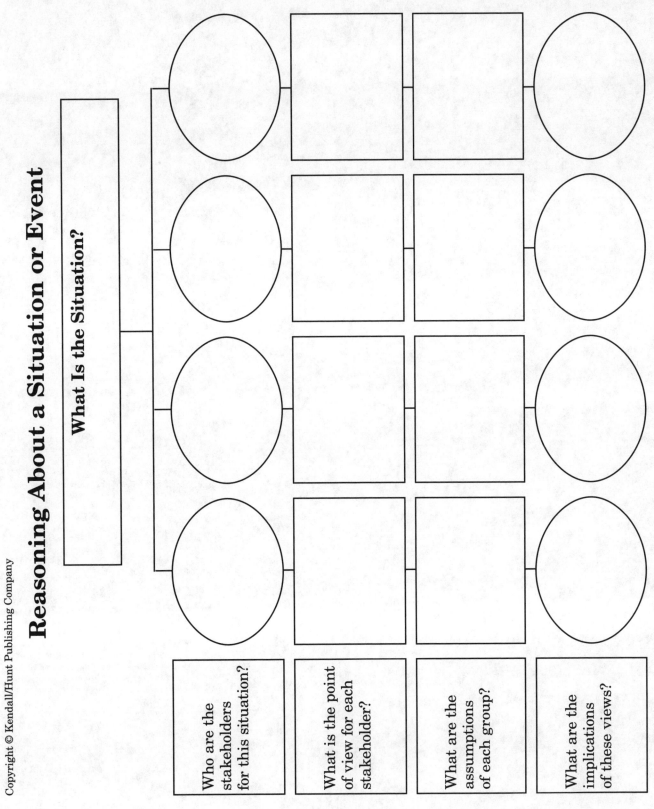

Who are the stakeholders for this situation?

What is the point of view for each stakeholder?

What are the assumptions of each group?

What are the implications of these views?

Name _____   Date _____

Observing the Effects of Tuberculosis

1. Observe normal lung tissue. Draw a picture of what you see and label its parts.

2. Observe tuberculosis-infected lung tissue. Draw a picture of what you see. How does the appearance of this tissue differ from the appearance of normal lung? How might the changes you see affect the function of the respiratory system?

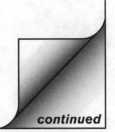

continued

3. Observe *M. tuberculosis.* Draw a picture of what you see and label its parts. Could you see *M. tuberculosis* bacilli in the diseased lung? Explain.

Name _____   Date _____

Information from Dr. Goldstein

Jason and Michael Miller, Todd's younger brothers, have both had positive tuberculin tests. Sputum smears are negative for acid-fast bacteria. Chest X-rays are pending, as are culture results. I have started both of them on rifampin and isoniazid.

Name _____ Date _____

Information from Mr. Miller

Todd's uncle, Jim Miller, and his aunt, Sarah Miller, have been contacted about Todd's illness and have been tested for TB. Both had positive tuberculin tests. Sputum smears from Sarah Miller were positive for acid-fast bacilli. Culture results and X-ray results are unavailable.

Name _____   Date _____

Information from Schoolwide Testing
at Eastbridge High School

Out of 1,435 students tested at Eastbridge High School, six have newly positive tuberculin tests. Three of these students are on the swim team; another is Todd Miller's girlfriend; and the remaining two students have no obvious connection to Todd Miller.

No faculty members had newly positive tuberculin tests.

Name _____   Date _____

Information from Schoolwide Testing
at Eastbridge Community Preschool

No students or teachers at the Eastbridge Community Preschool had newly positive tuberculin tests.

Information from Schoolwide Testing at Eastbridge Middle School

No students or teachers at Eastbridge Middle School had newly positive tuberculin tests.

Name _____ Date _____

Information from Dr. Goldstein

Jason and Michael Miller have both undergone chest X-rays; results were negative. Culture tests were negative for *M. tuberculosis* for both boys.

Name _____   Date _____

E-Mail from the Director of Public Health Department

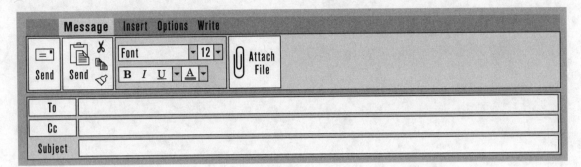

Susan,

I'll be very interested to hear how the testing went in the schools. Fax me the results as soon as you get them. Also, send me an action plan for what you'll be doing to follow up on these results.

The meeting has been great. I've been hearing the latest on emerging diseases—lots of fascinating new data! I'm going to be extending my trip by a week so I can go visit some friends at the National Institutes of Health. I'm sure that you'll be able to handle anything that comes up while I'm gone.

Marvin

Name _____   Date _____

Health Department Action Plan

1. Briefly describe the situation that requires action.

2. Why must the health department become involved in this situation?

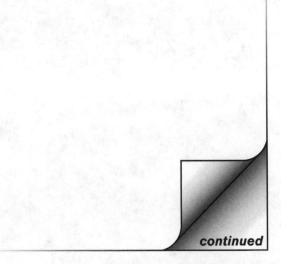

continued

3. What must be done? Give a good reason for each recommended action. Use another sheet if necessary.

   Action   **Reason**

   a.

   b.

   c.

4. Who outside the health department must be involved in the proposed activities? List people to contact and their roles in this plan. Use another sheet if necessary.

   Person   **Role**

   a.

   b.

   c.

Name _____   Date _____

The Eastbridge Gazette Editorial

In Our Opinion . . .

by Jim Erickson, Editor in Chief

The tuberculosis outbreak at Eastbridge High School is highly alarming. This contagious and dangerous disease is now threatening Americans anew as Third World conditions in America's inner cities act together to allow its reemergence.

Here in Eastbridge, most of us enjoy good medical care and an environment that is free of inner-city problems. Still, the spread of TB in our high school shows that even we are not safe from society's ills.

TB spreads best under crowded and unsanitary conditions. Eastbridge High School has been severely overcrowded for at least the last 5 years, and things will only get worse thanks to the unexpected but welcome growth in our city. It is time for the school board and Principal Smith to alleviate the unsanitary and dangerous conditions that allowed the spread of TB among our young people.

Name _____   Date _____

Problem Log Questions

1. Based on your lab results, how would you define "clean"? Explain your answer.

2. Is it necessary to eliminate all microorganisms in order to have a safe environment? Explain your answer.

Name _____   Date _____

Student Brainstorming Guide

1. What do we need to find out? (What is the scientific problem?)

2. What materials do we have available?

Cothron, J. G., Giese, R. N., & Rezba, R. J. (1989). *Students and research*. Dubuque, IA: Kendall/Hunt Publishing Co.

continued

3. How can we use these materials to help us find out?

4. What do we think will happen? (What is our hypothesis?)

5. What will we need to observe or measure in order to find out the answer to our scientific question?

Name _____ Date _____

Experimental Design Planner

Title of Experiment:

Hypothesis (Educated guess about what will happen):

Independent Variable (The variable that you change):

Dependent Variable (The variable that responds to changes in the independent variable):

Observations/Measurements to Make:

Constants (All the things or factors that remain the same):

Control (The standard for comparing experimental effects):

Name _____ Date _____

Experimental Protocol

1. List the materials you will need.

2. Write a step-by-step description of what you will do (like a recipe!). List every action you will take during the experiment.

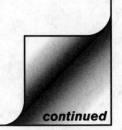

continued

3. What data will you be collecting?

4. Design a data table to record and analyze your information.

Name _____   Date _____

Laboratory Report

1. What did you do or test? (Include your experiment title.)

2. How did you do it? You can go back to your **Experimental Protocol** (Handout 10.3) and use the information from the first two questions.

3. What did you find out? (Include a data summary and the explanation of its meaning.)

continued

4. What did you learn from your experiment?

5. What additional questions do you now have?

6. Does the information you learned help with the problem?

Name _____ Date _____

Information from the Miller Family

Sarah Miller is concerned about the possibility that she may have been infected by one of her patients who is infected with a drug-resistant strain of the disease. Her physician has initiated tests to determine whether her TB is drug resistant.

Name _____   Date _____

Problem Log Questions

1. Based on his treatment plan for Todd Miller, what did Dr. Goldstein assume about Todd's *M. tuberculosis* bacteria? How do you know?

2. At present, doctors don't automatically test all newly diagnosed tuberculosis patients to see whether they are infected with drug-resistant tuberculosis.

   a. Give a good reason for automatically testing all tuberculosis patients to see if they are infected with drug-resistant tuberculosis.

continued

b. Give a good reason against automatically testing all tuberculosis patients to see if they are infected with drug-resistant tuberculosis.

c. Do you think it would be better to test all tuberculosis patients to see whether their bacilli are drug resistant or do you think it would be better to leave things as they are? Why?

E-Mail from Earl Smith, Principal
of Eastbridge High School

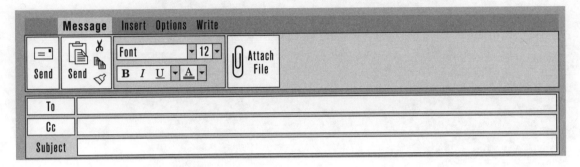

Susan,

The school nurse told me that some people are at greater risk of catching TB or having bad cases of it than others. She said that people who are taking chemotherapy are in danger of bad cases of TB. Our school secretary is taking chemotherapy for breast cancer. She has a very small office and sees students constantly. She's worried that these conditions are dangerous for her. Are they? What should we be doing to keep her safe?

Earl

Name _____   Date _____

E-Mail from Earl Smith

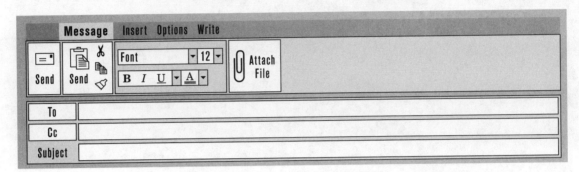

Susan,

A member of my staff has come to me in confidence and revealed that he is HIV positive. He is one of Todd Miller's teachers and is concerned about his own safety as well as the possibility that he could be a danger to his students if he comes down with TB. He does not yet have a primary care physician here in town and is concerned about confidentiality. While he had a tuberculin test when the health department visited the school and the test was negative, he knows that this may not mean anything in his case. What should I do about this?

Earl

Name _____   Date _____

Letter to *The Eastbridge Gazette* Editor

To the Editor:

The epidemic of TB at Eastbridge High should not have happened and wouldn't have happened if it weren't for the immorality of some Americans. We cleaned up this country in the fifties, and now thanks to drugs and AIDS and illegal immigrants, we've got a TB problem again. We should remember this when we vote in November.

Ira Stanley
Long-time resident of Eastbridge

Name _____   Date _____

E-Mail from John Erickson

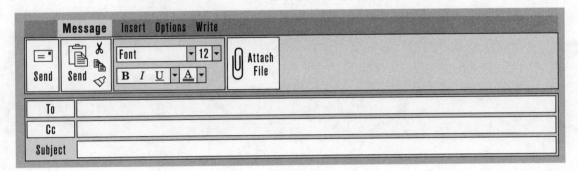

Susan,

I would appreciate it if you could respond to the letter to the editor that came out in today's paper. While I know that there are elements of truth in what Mr. Stanley said, I would like to print a more balanced and informed discussion of the subject in the next edition.

John Erickson
Editor of *The Eastbridge Gazette*

Name _____   Date _____

Field Trip Planning Guide

Brainstorming Questions

1. What kind of a place do we need to visit?

2. What do we want to find out at this place?

Logistics: Planning

1. Where are we going?

2. Whom do we need to contact in order to arrange a visit?

3. Who will set up the visit?

4. Who needs to go?

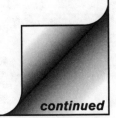

continued

Logistics: Firm Plans

1. When are we going?

2. How are we going to get there?

3. Who is our host?

4. Have we talked to our host about why we want to visit and what we want to learn?

Sensitivity Issues

1. How will the people there feel about having us visit?

2. How should we behave in order to respect their feelings?

Name _____ Date _____

Problem Log Questions

1. Was the trip useful?

2. What was the most interesting piece of new information you gleaned from the trip?

3. How did you feel about the trip?

Name _____   Date _____

Visitor Planning Sheet

Name of Visitor:_____

Who is this visitor?

_____

_____

_____

Why is this visitor coming to see us?

_____

_____

Why is this visitor important to us?

_____

_____

_____

What would you like to tell our visitor about our problem?

_____

_____

What questions do you want to ask the visitor?

_____

_____

_____

Name _____ Date _____

Problem Log Questions

1. Did you learn anything that would help you know how to solve the problem? What was it, and how is it helpful?

2. What did you find most interesting about the speaker's presentation? Why?

Name _____   Date _____

Memo from the Miller Family

MEMO

Sarah Miller's culture test results have come back. Her TB is not multi-drug-resistant. Both she and her husband are responding well to treatment.

Name   Date

E-Mail to the Director of Public Health Department

New Information on Testing

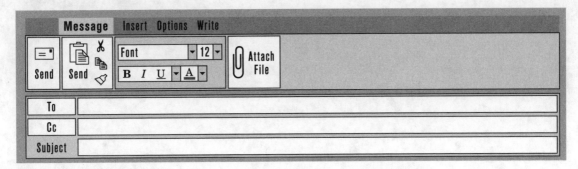

Marvin,

The last testing of contacts in the TB situation has been completed. No additional cases of TB have been found. We will, of course, continue to monitor the situation closely.

Susan Ostrovsky

Name _____ Date _____

Memo from Earl Smith

MEMO

Susan,

The school board and I have come under considerable political pressure to come up with a set of changes to implement at the high school that would prevent another TB epidemic. We would appreciate any recommendations that you would have.

We will be having our last board meeting of the year a week from tonight. Could you please make a list of recommendations and present them at the board meeting? For obvious reasons, we would like a copy of your statement, preferably before the meeting, so that we can prepare an appropriately supportive response. You will have approximately 15 minutes to make your presentation.

Earl

P.S. For financial reasons, it will be impossible to build a second high school or add permanent space to Eastbridge High for at least 5 years. As you know, the voters defeated the last school bond proposal. So, we'll have to accommodate at least 500 more students than the school was designed to handle for at least the next few years; projections from the mayor's office indicate that the number of excess students could be more like 700 by the time we can afford to build a second high school. This means that while you can recommend immediate expansion, we won't be able to follow up on it. We'll need other options as well.

Name _____   Date _____

Susan's List: Possible Tuberculosis Control Measures

What to do	**How this will help**	**References (at least two)**
1.		
2.		
3.		

Name _____   Date _____

Problem Log Questions

1. What was the most important thing you learned during this unit, and why?

2. If you could change one thing about this unit, what would it be? Why do you say this?

Name _____   Date _____

Content Post-Assessment

1. a. Why is tuberculosis especially dangerous to people who are immunodeficient?

   b. List two groups of people who are especially at risk if they become infected with tuberculosis.

2. a. How does the tuberculin test work?

   b. Is the tuberculin skin test a good way to find out if someone has active tuberculosis? Why or why not?

   c. Why don't tuberculin tests work in AIDS patients?

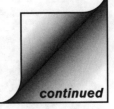

continued

3. Describe a method that could be used to determine whether bacteria are resistant to ampicillin (a commonly used antibiotic). What materials would you need to do the test, how would you do it, and what would you expect to see if the bacteria were indeed resistant to ampicillin?

4. Describe the functions of each of the following immune system cells:

B cells

T cells

Macrophages

Name   Date

Experimental Design Post-Assessment A

Construct a fair test of the following question: What cleaning procedure is most effective for decontaminating a dirty food preparation area?

Describe in detail how you would test this question. Be as scientific as you can as you write about your test. Write the steps you would take to determine which cleaning procedure is most effective for decontaminating a dirty food preparation area.

Adapted from Fowler, M. (1990). The diet cola test. *Science Scope, 13(4)*, 32–34.

Name _____   Date _____

Experimental Design Post-Assessment B

You have asthma, a chronic disease that makes you cough (which is annoying but not necessarily serious) and makes it hard to breathe (which is serious); severe asthma attacks can be life threatening. Most of the time, you have no problems and manage to get by without using bronchodilators (drugs that expand the size of your breathing passages and relieve your asthma symptoms). You are very allergic to ragweed: ragweed pollen makes your asthma much worse. During ragweed season, which typically lasts about 6 weeks where you live, you find that you need to use bronchodilators much more frequently. Your biggest problems are at night: the inhaled bronchodilator that you use at bedtime wears off by about 2:00 A.M., and so you wake up coughing, have to take another dose from your inhaler, and then have trouble getting back to sleep. Your allergist suggests that you try an oral form of the medication that may take longer to wear off. She cautions you not to use the oral form during an acute asthma attack, though, because it takes 20 minutes to start working, whereas your inhaled bronchodilator only takes a few seconds. How can you decide which form of the medication works best for you at night during ragweed season?

1. Describe an experiment that would allow you to choose between the two. In your answer, include the following:

   a. Your hypothesis

   b. The materials you would need (including any necessary safety equipment)

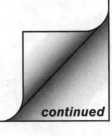

continued

c. The protocol you would use

d. A data table showing what data you would collect

e. A description of how you would use your data to decide whether the oral form of your bronchodilator works better than the inhaled form

Name _____   Date _____

Systems Post-Assessment

A classroom can be thought of as a system.

1. List the parts of the system in the spaces provided. Include boundaries, elements, inputs, and outputs.

   Boundaries:

   Elements:

   Inputs:

   Outputs:

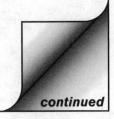

continued

2. Draw a diagram of the system that shows where each of the parts can be found.

3. On your diagram, draw lines (in a different color) showing three important interactions between different parts of the classroom system. Why is each of these interactions important to the system? Explain your answer.

   a. Interaction 1

   b. Interaction 2

   c. Interaction 3